NATIONAL GEOGRAPHIC

T0042393

Sweet HARVEST

PIONEER EDITION

By Dana Jensen and Adele Conover

CONTENTS

Nature's C

andy

By Dana Jensen

Who likes candy? Everyone, it seems. Candy is full of sugar. The sugar makes it sweet. You can find sugar in other foods, too. Many cereals have sugar. Juices have sugar. Soda often has sugar as well.

Where does all that sugar come from? Look at the picture on the left for a hint.

Popular Plant

The boys in the photo are holding a plant called sugarcane. Most sugar comes from juices inside this plant.

Sugarcane needs 8 to 22 months to **ripen**. It needs lots of water. It needs sunshine. It needs rich dirt.

The sugarcane grows taller. The juice inside grows sweeter. Workers wait for the juice to become very sweet. Then they cut down the sugarcane.

Machines press out the juice. Workers boil the juice in big pots. Machines separate tiny grains from the juice. These are sugar grains.

Chew on This!

Trees give us treats, too. When tree bark is cut, **sap** runs out. Have you seen sap? It is sticky. It is like gum.

Thousands of years ago, people chewed the sap of some trees. They used it like gum. Native Americans and other people liked it.

Over time, people found ways to make gum taste better. Today we add sugar to gum. We add mint taste. We add fruit flavors. We sometimes make gum in wild colors. Yet all our chewing gum started with sap.

The Chocolate Tree

Trees also give us chocolate. Cacao (kuh KOW) trees grow fruit with seeds, or beans, inside. People scoop the beans out. Then they let them sit. The beans' flavor changes. Next, workers roast the beans and grind them. That makes chocolate powder.

Long ago, people mixed the powder with water. It was a bitter drink. Over time, people added sugar and milk. That makes chocolate taste good.

So when you have sugar, gum, or chocolate, remember this. Nature can be pretty sweet!

Sweet Job. *A worker picks fruit from a cacao tree in Malaysia. Then workers open the fruit. They take out the seeds.*

Sticky Business

These workers in Mexico make gum the traditional way—by hand.

Drip. A worker cuts a tree. Sticky sap pours out. The sap will become gum.

Strain. Workers pour the white sap through a strainer. This removes dirt.

Stretch. A worker stirs the sap. It becomes stretchy. It turns into gum.

Squeeze. A worker puts the gum into a box. Later, workers cut the gum into pieces.

From Bean to Bar

Chocolate begins as the seeds of cacao pods. These seeds are called beans. But the raw beans do not taste good. It takes many steps today to turn bitter beans into a yummy chocolate bar.

1 First, you pick the cacao pods. You take out the raw seeds, or beans.

2 You let the beans ferment, or change. Then you dry the beans.

3 Then you roast the beans. You break them up. This makes cacao nibs.

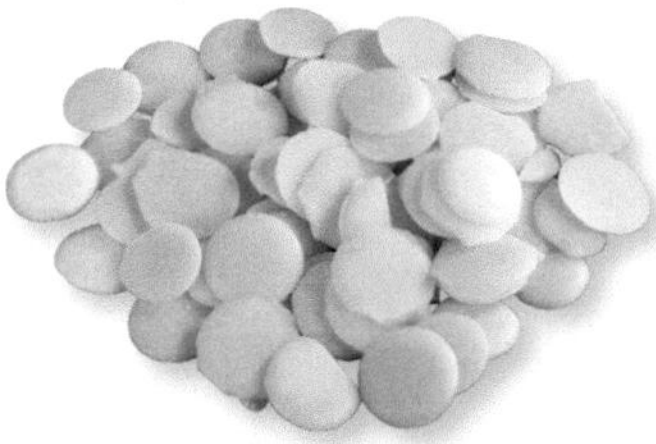

4 Next, you grind up the nibs. This makes cacao paste.

5 Then you add sugar to make chocolate. Or you press the paste to make cocoa butter and cocoa powder.

6 Now, you are ready to make milk chocolate. Mix the cocoa butter and cocoa powder with milk and sugar.

7 Finally, you shape the mixture into chocolate bars.

Cool Beans. *Chocolate is made from the seeds inside a cacao pod.*

PASS THE CHOCOLATE

By Adele Conover

One day your mother says, "Eat your chocolate. It's good for you." Are you surprised? Scientists are not. They know that chocolate is good for you. It has stuff like **vitamins** in it. Take out the sugar. Takc out the fat. What is left of your chocolate bar? Things that are good for your heart. Things that are good for your blood.

The stuff in chocolate is a lot like vitamin C. Vitamin C is good for you. It keeps bad things from hurting your body. It keeps your arteries healthy. Arteries carry blood away from the heart. The stuff in chocolate may even fight cancer. No one knows for sure. The research is not finished.

Bitter Beginnings

The first chocolate was made thousands of years ago from cacao trees in the rain forests of Central America. Cacao trees have **pods** on their trunks. The pods are yellow or red. The pods have hard shells.

Humans used the seeds for food. First they ground the seeds into powder. Next, they mixed the powder with hot water. It became a chocolate drink. The drink was bitter. They mixed in vanilla and chili peppers!

The First Chocolate Lovers

Most scientists think they know who made chocolate first. They were the Olmec. These ancient people lived about 3,000 years ago. They lived on the coast of Central America.

Making the Cut. *A worker uses a knife to cut off a cacao pod.*

Full of Beans. *This is the inside of a cacao pod. White fruit covers the dark seeds.*

The Medicine Drink

The next people to use chocolate were the Maya. They lived around 600 C.E. They grew cacao trees. Only men drank the chocolate. They took it to cure stomachaches and to get well from diseases.

The Aztec people drank chocolate, too. They lived in central Mexico. They called their chocolate drink, *xocoatl* (shoh KOH hat). They also took it as medicine. They thought cacao seeds were valuable. They even used them for money.

Chocolate Goes to Spain

In 1519, the Aztec king Moctezuma gave some *xocoatl* to Spanish explorer Hernán Cortés. Cortés wrote to the king of Spain. He said "a cup of this precious drink permits a man to walk a whole day without food."

In 1528 Cortés took cacao seeds to Spain. The Spanish added sugar to their *xocoatl*. It tasted sweet. The Spanish kept their way of making chocolate a secret. More than 80 years went by. Then more people in Europe learned how to make the drink.

THE STORY OF CHOCOLATE

1000 B.C.E. The Olmec people grow cacao trees in Central America.

600 C.E. The Maya use cacao seeds. They make a chocolate drink.

1519 The Aztec king meets Hernán Cortés and gives him a chocolate drink.

1528 Cortés takes the chocolate drink to Spain. He teaches the Spanish how to make it. They add sugar. They keep the recipe a secret.

1600s All of Europe learns the secret.

Main Squeeze. *This machine squeezes out chocolate. The chocolate hardens quickly.*

Junk Food or Health Food?

Soon the love of chocolate spread across all Europe. There was a Dutch chocolate maker. He lived in the early 1700s and invented a machine. It pressed chocolate into "cakes." Soon, these cakes became our candy bars.

Today, scientists and chocolate makers try to make chocolate bars that are healthy. They want to make them with less fat and sugar. If they can, people might not call chocolate bars junk food anymore.

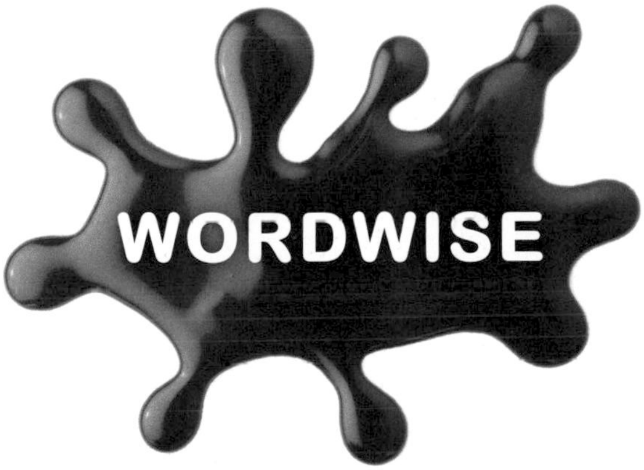

pod: a container for seeds that grows on some plants

ripen: to become ready to eat

sap: sticky liquid inside a plant

vitamin: something in food you need to stay healthy

1657 Stores in England sell solid chocolate. People make it into a drink. Shops sell the new drink all over Europe.

1700s The English add milk to their hot chocolate drink.

1765 The first U.S. chocolate factory is built.

1900 U.S. chocolate makers use a milk chocolate recipe to make candy bars.

2010s The average American eats 12 pounds of chocolate a year.

Sweet Endings

Bite into some treats from nature.
Then answer these questions.

1. What does sugarcane need to grow? How long does sugarcane take to get ripe?
2. What two kinds of candy are made from trees? What parts of the tree are they made from?
3. How do people make gum the traditional way? List the steps in order.
4. How did people first eat chocolate?
5. What events have changed the way people eat chocolate? How are they related?